Kiama AND THE Stubborn Cow

by Otis Greene
illustrated by Christian Slade

Harcourt
SCHOOL PUBLISHERS

Copyright © by Harcourt, Inc.

All rights reserved. No part of this publication may be reproduced or transmitted in any form or by any means, electronic or mechanical, including photocopy, recording, or any information storage and retrieval system, without permission in writing from the publisher.

Requests for permission to make copies of any part of the work should be addressed to School Permissions and Copyrights, Harcourt, Inc., 6277 Sea Harbor Drive, Orlando, Florida 32887-6777. Fax: 407-345-2418.

HARCOURT and the Harcourt Logo are trademarks of Harcourt, Inc., registered in the United States of America and/or other jurisdictions.

Printed in China

ISBN 10: 0-15-350514-1
ISBN 13: 978-0-15-350514-0

Ordering Options
ISBN 10: 0-15-350334-3 (Grade 4 Below-Level Collection)
ISBN 13: 978-0-15-350334-4 (Grade 4 Below-Level Collection)
ISBN 10: 0-15-357503-4 (package of 5)
ISBN 13: 978-0-15-357503-7 (package of 5)

If you have received these materials as examination copies free of charge, Harcourt School Publishers retains title to the materials and they may not be resold. Resale of examination copies is strictly prohibited and is illegal.

Possession of this publication in print format does not entitle users to convert this publication, or any portion of it, into electronic format.

2 3 4 5 6 7 8 9 10   985   12 11 10 09 08 07

"Come on, Kianna, let's go out and enjoy our summer vacation," said her friend Tania.

"I don't want to," replied Kianna, as she continued to leaf through a magazine.

"It's not so hot out today, so we can jump rope!" begged Carley, Kianna's other friend.

"I don't have to go out if I don't want to," replied Kianna. Tania and Carley sighed.

"Well, I guess we'll be leaving then," said Carley, and she and Tania marched out the front door.

Chicago summers can get very hot, but today was quite cool and pleasant. Carley and Tania were eager to enjoy the nice weather while they could. Besides, they said, they had been inside at school all year, and now they were free to play.

Kianna was just being her stubborn self. Carley and Tania had been her friends since first grade, and they were used to her stubborn ways, but they certainly didn't enjoy them.

"Hi, Mom," said Kianna when her mother returned from work later that day.

"Hi, baby. This is from your cousin Jan," said her mom. She handed Kianna a letter, and Kianna immediately felt a surge of excitement.

"Jan invited me to spend some time with her this summer at the ranch where she works!" said Kianna. Jan was twenty-one. She went to college in Texas and worked at a cattle ranch there in the summer. Kianna's mother took the letter and read it over carefully.

"Well, Kianna, I'm a little reluctant to let you go there," her mother said with a concerned look on her face. "You're used to playing out on the sidewalk and walking over to the corner grocery store here in the city. What do *you* know about living on a ranch?" her mother asked.

"Mom, I'll be fine, and Jan will look after me," she begged.

"Well, maybe it'll be good for you, and maybe you can learn something there. I'll give Jan a call," her mom decided.

One week later, Kianna and her mother rode the bus to Union Station in downtown Chicago. From there, Kianna would take a train to Texas.

Kianna's mom had arranged for Kianna to travel on the train alone. The train conductor talked to Kianna's mom and assured her that Kianna would have a safe ride to Austin, Texas.

Kianna gazed out the window as the train left the station and thought about what it would be like to live and work on a ranch.

Before Kianna knew it, the train had arrived in Texas, and she was at the ranch. The Triple B Ranch was enormous. The countryside was flat and dry, and there were huge fields where the cattle grazed.

Jan showed Kianna around. Kianna would sleep on the floor in a sleeping bag in Jan's room.

"Now listen, Kianna," Jan said seriously. "This isn't like playing jump rope in the city. You have to be tough out here, and you have to work hard, okay?"

"Okay!" said Kianna enthusiastically.

On her first full day of "work" on the ranch, Jan warned, "Kianna, whenever you walk around out here, watch your step because sometimes there are snakes lurking around."

Kianna looked at the ground nervously as she followed Jan around to the front of the barn. "Now we have to inspect the horses to make certain they are healthy so that they can work," explained Jan.

Later that morning, Kianna helped Jan untangle some ropes. "We'll need these when we have to move the cows," Jan said.

Kianna got used to working on the ranch and started to become a little more comfortable around the animals. One day, Kianna and Jan walked out to a large corral with their ropes. "We have to transfer these cows into the next corral, and since they usually follow the lead cow, we just need to get her to start walking," explained Jan.

Kianna watched as Jan coaxed most of the cows into the other corral. One cow, which had a rumpled hide, would not move.

Jan roped it and handed the end of the rope to Kianna. "Okay, get her moving," said Jan.

Kianna pulled hard on the rope, making it taut, but the cow wouldn't move. The cow just looked at her and stayed put.

"Try talking to it calmly while pulling on the rope," Jan suggested.

"Okay, cow, here we go," said Kianna in a soothing voice. The cow didn't move an inch. "Are you just going to stay here all day?" she said to the cow.

Suddenly, Kianna heard the words of Tania resound through her head: "*Come on, let's go out and enjoy our summer vacation.*" There in the hot sun of Texas, Kianna realized something. "I'm kind of like this cow," she thought. "I get stubborn, and then no one can make me do anything I don't want to do."

Then she said to Jan, "This cow sure is stubborn."

"That's pretty annoying, isn't it?" asked Jan.

"It sure is," said Kianna. Now she understood how her friends felt when she was stubborn.

Kianna returned home after a wonderful month on the ranch. Her mother met her at the train station. On the ride home, Kianna told her mom all the interesting things she had learned in Texas. "Mom, do you know that sometimes cows can be really stubborn and not move?"

"Stubborn? Hmm, that sounds kind of familiar," said her mother, chuckling.

"Actually, that's another thing I learned, Mom, not to be so stubborn," said Kianna seriously.

"Well, I'm glad to hear that, honey," replied her mom.

A week later, Kianna, Tania, and Carley were jumping rope outside. "It's hot, so how about we go get something to drink?" suggested Tania.

"No, let's jump a little more," answered Kianna.

"Come on, Kianna. Can't you just—"

"You're absolutely right," said Kianna, cutting her off immediately. "Let's go get some water." Tania and Carley just stared at Kianna in amazement. They were expecting her to be stubborn again, but Kianna just looked at them and smiled proudly.

Think Critically

1. What problem did Kianna have? What helped her solve it?

2. At what time of year does this story take place?

3. What is the setting at the beginning of the story? How does it change throughout the story?

4. What word means almost the same thing as *taut* does on page 11?

5. What are some details from this story that interested you?

 **Social Studies**

Make a Map Look at a map of the United States, and draw your own map of Kianna's route from Chicago, Illinois, to Austin, Texas. What other states would Kianna have traveled through? Add the states to your map.

School-Home Connection Tell a family member about this story. Then have a discussion about ways that people can solve their problems.

Word Count: 1,009